THIS GIRL DID

ALICE KYARIMPA

STORY TERRACE

© Copyright 2022 - All rights reserved.

The content contained within this book may not be reproduced, duplicated, or transmitted without direct written permission from the author or the publisher.

Under no circumstances will any blame or legal responsibility be held against the publisher, or author, for any damages, reparation, or monetary loss due to the information contained within this book, either directly or indirectly.

Legal Notice:

This book is copyright protected. It is only for personal use. You cannot amend, distribute, sell, use, quote or paraphrase any part, or the content within this book, without the consent of the author or publisher.

Disclaimer Notice:

Please note the information contained within this document is for educational and entertainment purposes only. All effort has been executed to present accurate, up to date, reliable, complete information. No warranties of any kind are declared or implied. Readers acknowledge that the author is not engaged in the rendering of legal, financial, medical or professional advice. The content within this book has been derived from various sources. Please consult a licensed professional before attempting any techniques outlined in this book.

By reading this document, the reader agrees that under no circumstances is the author responsible for any losses, direct or indirect, that are incurred as a result of the use of the information contained within this document, including, but not limited to, errors, omissions, or inaccuracies.

CONTENTS

1. The Terror of Nightfall   1
2. Who'd want to be a girl?   7
3. Bananas are my business!   15
4. Nine Years of Abuse   21
5. Loving London, Loving Life   25
6. Double joy, singular heartbreak   29
7. The Power of Positivity!   33

About the Author   35

I would like to dedicate this book to my lovely Mother Florence Mubonehe born 1938-2016 who never went to school and was dedicated to educating all her children both girls and a boy. To my beloved Twins Abigail and Joshua who will later be reading my stories. They are a handful, and do drive me crazy at times, but fill me with joy every moment. To my sisters Anna Ruth Phebby and my brother Nicholas. Thanks Alice

1

THE TERROR OF NIGHTFALL

'Give us the money, or we shoot!'

I couldn't see which of the six soldiers had shouted out to my mum and my uncle. It was growing dark, and our very basic house had no electricity. All I could see were their guns – long, metal rifles held in the hands of bulky, sweaty men in army green government uniforms who now filled our tiny house in Kabale with terror. They spoke in both English, then and now the official language of Uganda, and Swahili (a common language in East Africa, which was learnt by men during their army training, and so spoken really only by them). My mother couldn't understand a word. She was raised in a rural village on the shores of Lake Bunyonyi and only spoke the local dialect. She went to stand in front of me and my two younger sisters, Anna and Ruth, ready to use her body to protect us. We were aged just eight, seven and three.

Then, two of the men seized my uncle: they grabbed my mother's older brother and pulled him out of the house. I heard a scuffle and then a sound that could have been guns firing.

Next, the remaining soldiers turned their attention to Mum – two of them grabbed her, and the final two followed them out of the house. Mum didn't make a sound as she left, and I wonder now if she had decided to accept whatever her fate might be if that would mean her children were saved.

'Alice, what are we going to do?' sobbed my sisters.

'We're going to pray,' I said.

Uganda was under the dictatorship of Idi Amin, and a nightly curfew was in place. Even so, every night, peaceable civilians were violated on the streets or in their homes. Women and young girls were raped or kidnapped and then raped. Men were captured and forced to join the army. Those with money were robbed. Some people were murdered, seemingly without reason. It was a desperate time to be a single mother with a young family.

We were poor and kept our heads down. Even so, for the previous few weeks, we'd left our house every evening before dusk to hide outside in the bush so that soldiers couldn't find and attack us. As it grew cold, we'd huddle up by trees under just one shared blanket. Other families would be close by doing the same. In the morning, we'd return home, and I'd change into my school skirt and top. But this particular evening, we'd stayed at home a bit later because my uncle had popped round to see us. He ran a small grocery store, and we saw him now and again. He was just getting by, but it could be that the soldiers thought he had some money.

Now, with my terrified sisters looking to me for hope, I sat down on the floor and made my young voice sound older and calmer than I felt as I prayed aloud.

'Please, God. Don't let these men kill our mum. She is all we have in our lives. I can't take on the responsibility of caring for my sisters. Not yet.'

After what seemed forever but was perhaps an hour at most, Mum reappeared, still with the soldiers. She was crying, and her body shook as she went straight into her bedroom, then emerged carrying a small purse. She opened it, and a soldier took every note and coin that was inside. And then the men left.

After that, Mum pulled us all close, and we cuddled together in the bedroom. When I woke the next morning, she had collected together the few blankets and clothes we had. 'We leave now,' she told my sisters and me. 'It's not safe to stay here, plus all the money I had for rent or for food has gone. I cannot look after you anymore. So today, we begin a new plan.'

That plan involved walking eight hours to my grandmother's thatched hut. There, my mum would tell her mother that she believed her brother had been killed. (And in truth, we never saw or heard from him again). Then, she would leave us and walk the eight hours back to the town because it was the only way she could keep on working and keep alive her dream that her daughters would not lead the life that she had.

I will never know whether or not the soldiers sexually assaulted my mother that day. When I was old enough to understand these things, the shock of speculating what might have happened was dreadful.

My incredible, amazing mother never went to school because her parents (and parents throughout my home country) believed that girls were good only for cultivating the land, clearing up after their brothers – and being sold as soon after puberty as possible into marriage. This was because the man's family would give the girl's family several cows in return. And the girl's family needed those cows, not just for milk because everyone was poor, but so that they would have something to offer another girl's family when it was time for their sons to take wives.

My incredible, amazing mother, who could never read or write, devoted her life to ensuring that I would go to school. It was her mission that my sisters and I would learn to read and write and so might discover that girls deserve to, and are capable of, taking control of their lives. That we have all gone on to gain university degrees, own our own homes and have the strength to choose partners who love and respect us or refuse those that do not is due to her legacy.

My incredible, amazing mother was called Florence Mubonehe (born on 7th August 1938). Very tragically, she died on 4th February 2016, and the funeral was on 6th February, eight days before I became a mother myself. So I couldn't share with her how being blessed with twins (a boy and a girl) has enabled me to parent, with true equality, right from day one.

I am proud to dedicate my story to my incredible, amazing mother.

I want to share my story with as wide an audience as I can reach. As well as being born into extreme poverty in a turbulent, violent time, I have gone on to endure an arranged relationship with a controlling, abusive man. I have had to escape with nothing to begin a new life halfway across the world. Yet today, I hold two master's degrees and a professional job; I own a property in central London, and each day I wake up in comfort and safety as the joyful sounds of my children fill our home. I am also CEO of a charity I founded that has set up a school in Uganda for vulnerable children.

As you read my story, you will hear how it was to live in terror and in hunger – and to be so desperate that you could not be sure which was the worse cross to bear. There will also be tough memories from when I was trapped in an abusive relationship and how I found the courage to break free. But what I hope you will take most from my story is the power of perseverance, persistence and patience.

I was 43 years old when I became pregnant with Abigail and Joshua. Forty-three! After more than 20 years of believing this could never happen! I am a Christian, and on a personal level, I believe that my prayers were answered. Yet, whether you have faith or not, I truly believe that a good life is there for *everyone* who has courage and resilience and who leads a life that differentiates right from wrong. Because of what happened to me, I care most of all about the extra injustices women may face. If my story inspires even one woman to keep on going, push harder in the face of rejection or break free from abuse when there appears no way out – then I will have succeeded.

I write this with warmth and true sincerity of purpose, and thank you for reading my story.

Easter 2022
Alice Kyarimpa
London, England

2

WHO'D WANT TO BE A GIRL?

For centuries, African culture has celebrated when the first child is a boy – and commiserated when a girl arrives instead. Even in the 1970s, when I was born, many women became outcasts because they'd committed the misfortune of child number one being female. They might be banned from social events; their families (and even their husbands!) might disown them to create a situation that would only be rectified if they then went on to have a boy.

My mother had the extra embarrassment (in her parents' eyes) of having eloped with a man from outside of her village. But at least her parents were embarrassed rather than unhinged. Such was the shame afforded to illegitimacy that now and again, there would be rumours about how another pregnant, unmarried woman was murdered and thrown into Lake Bunyoni by her own family. None of these rumoured murders would be investigated by police. It was just how life was then. My grandparents' solution was to stop speaking to their daughter, which they kept to for at least five years.

When she was around 18, Mum had met Nathan Rutukura, an

anaesthetist at the Leprosy Hospital at Bwama Island, where they both worked. He'd started talking to her one day, whilst she was on a break from work. She was attractive and he was charming. After a sad childhood, Mum had found the courage to leave home and found a cleaning job at this hospital on the other side of Lake Bunyoni. The hospital was run by missionaries, and they had shown this eager, hard-working young girl kindness and helped her find a room nearby to live in.

As the only girl in her family, Mum's expected lot was that she would simply skivvy after her brothers, then be married off as soon as someone suitable was identified. Since early childhood, she'd spent her days tending to the family's crops and cleaning and preparing meals for her brothers. The worst bit wasn't the monotony or the long hours, but that she wasn't allowed to go to school. Often, she'd try to follow her brothers as they set off from their mud house to walk to school. But her mother or father would come out with a stick to insist that she return – and then beat her as punishment for trying to get an education.

Now and again, on Sundays, she did manage to break free from the compound where she lived. Local missionaries ran an outdoor Sunday class for both boys and girls. As well as hearing about the Bible, the missionaries did what they could to teach children to read and write. They had no paper or pens, so Mum learnt how to write her name in soil on the dry, hot earth. When she tried to share what she'd learnt with her family, no one wanted to know. Girls, she'd been told, could not have the happy life of boys and men. They were second – no, make that third-class citizens.

Now, in a relationship with a well-educated man, Mum thought she would be able to embrace a different future, a life alongside a partner who cared for her. Nathan was ambitious and secured a role as a senior anaesthetist at the regional hospital in Kabale. Mum went too – and I arrived on 24th October 1971, shortly before her 20th birthday.

In Uganda, only rich families pass the surname of the father onto their children. Everyone else is given two (or more!) names that are unique to them. Nathan was at the start of his career, so I wasn't given the Rutukura name. Besides, my sex made me a disappointment when I was born. Not to my wonderful mum, of course! Kyarimpa means 'what God will give me'. She was delighted to have a girl. After all, in her act of defying her parents' wishes that she stay home and wait to be 'sold' into marriage, she was already showing that girls didn't have to have a small, pre-decided life.

For my father, however, disappointment continued with the births of his next children. My sisters Anna, Ruth and Phebby appeared over the next decade. He didn't share this disappointment openly with us – he'd play games, give us sweets – but it was all an act, something he put on for a few hours when, late at night, he came to visit. Because that's the sorry truth about my father – while he lured Mum in by being charming and loving, he never committed to her at all. My parents never truly lived together; Dad simply visited whensoever it suited him. Even before Anna arrived, he was scarcely there. To all effects and purposes, Mum was left alone, a rural village girl, in a one-bedroom house in a city where she knew no one, and most people didn't even speak the same local dialect as her. She couldn't go home or even share what was happening with her family because they had rejected her too.

Far from being the charming, loving man he had presented as they courted, my father revealed himself to be an abusive man. Mum worked out that what had been a love match for her was just a relationship of convenience for him. Her role was to satisfy him sexually, as he demanded, and bear his children.

Although not married, Mum looked on herself as his wife. She believes that the next woman he got involved with also considered herself his wife too - although in fact my father never officially married anyone .This second 'wife' was not to be the last long-term on–off partner that Nathan took. Years later, we learnt that we had eight stepsisters and two stepbrothers as a result of these other 'secret' families.

What might have ruined other women made my incredible mum stronger. Phebby had arrived by now, so now there were four children to support. 'You girls are not going to have the same life as me,' she'd tell us as she shared what little food she'd been able to buy. 'You girls are going to be educated!' She'd pronounce this with certainty as she divided up the maize porridge of beans ('bins') and sweet potatoes that were our cheap, staple diet. When she hadn't been able to buy enough to fill four bowls of hot plain food, it was Mum who went without out. She managed to be able to cope with going hungry herself – goodness knows how. As well as looking after us, she put in a very full day's work at the hospital as a clerk.

Among my earliest memories is being carried on her back. When I was around three, she began to drop me off at a church nursery on her way to work. Anna would have been on her back instead by then! Even Mum couldn't manage a baby and a toddler and work. She'd hold my hand tight as we walked up the steep hill to the nursery. 'You learn up every scrap of knowledge they tell you, Alice,' she'd say. 'If you learn to read and write – anything is possible!'

The nursery was run by a church, and initially, it was free. When it began charging a small fee, Mum put in even more work hours so that I could go. Sometimes, we'd stop at the crossroads on the way. 'Just think – a daughter of mine will be able to read these,' she'd say, pointing up at road signs that showed the routes to different towns or even to the hospital where she worked.

The teachers at the nursery were kind, but no one said that I would ever amount to anything in life. It was all about survival. In overcrowded classes, it was rote learning to get to grips with the alphabet and basic mathematics.

One of the hardest things was concentrating through hunger. When you are born into the level of poverty that I was, it is hard to explain how the angry gnaw in your stomach roars louder than everything else that is going on. There was little joy in my childhood, not because I wasn't loved, but because it was a childhood of survival. I had no holidays, no celebrations and no toys were bought for me. At home, my sisters and I woke up hungry and frequently went to bed just the same. We were fortunate in that we were healthy and robust. Sickness was rife. In the village where my mother grew up, more than half of the children born would die before the age of two, typically from malnutrition or dehydration.

Because it was so unsafe, we seldom played outside. So I don't know how we managed to find the discarded banana leaves to make dolls out of, but one day we did. Another time – incredibly – we worked together to build a bicycle out of dried plant stems. I kid you not! And it was strong enough to ride on if you went downhill! It only lasted a few weeks, of course – but what a contrast in every way to the two beautiful bicycles I would go on to present to my children the Christmas they turned five. Whenever I compare my life as a child to the lifestyle that I give to my children, the contrasts are enough to bring tears to my eyes. Yet, amidst all the differences, there is one thing that they and I do have as a shared experience: a loving mum at the centre of everything.

I started at Kabale Demonstration School when I was around six years old. I found I had a quick, keen brain and loved my lessons. 'We must always find the money for school,' Mum said. 'Better to be in school and just have one meal a day than have two meals a day but not be able to pay for school.'

Occasionally, mum would have a day when she didn't work. It was on one of these days that she took us for what seemed the longest walk of my young life.

Four hours into that walk, I saw an elderly woman with a basket come into view.

'Grandma! Is that really you!'

I can't guarantee it was the first time I ever saw her, but it has become the first time that I remember. I looked across the bare, dry landscape, and just coming over the brow of a hill, I saw how this elderly woman had the same long, striding walk as my mother.

Even though I'd been on my small feet for four hours already, I sprinted the 100 or so yards to her. I wanted to reach her – and I was desperate to see what fruit and other wonderful items she might have for our picnic!

I had been around six years old when Mum and Grandma resumed speaking – and once they had, it was as if they had always been in touch. We'd meet up now and again – and what an adventure that was! In 1970s Uganda, there were practically no cars or buses. There was no railway line in our district either. People walked for hours. Distances between places were measured in walking hours. My grandmother's village was an eight-hour walk. We'd meet in the middle – but first, of course, it had to be arranged. There were no telephones in private homes (or my grandmother's entire village), and sending a letter was out when no one could read. Instead, you'd find someone who was going to your home village – and get them to pass on your message.

You would ask them to pass on something simple like, 'let's meet on Tuesday'. After a few days, you'd try to catch that same person again to check for a reply to your message. Then, come Tuesday, you'd both start walking at daybreak – and hope for the best!

The message carriers were working-age people who each day walked that incredible distance between village and town in order to keep a job. Clearly, they walked more quickly than me, but even so, they must have walked at least six hours, put in a day's work, and then walked six hours home. Tough, tough times.

It was one thing meeting my grandmother for delicious picnics – it was another to live with her, as my sisters and I had to after the dreadful day when my uncle was abducted by gunpoint in front of us.

I missed Mum; of course, I did. I missed school terribly, too – and I became terrified that I might never see either again. But something even more frightening was on my mind too.

A generation had passed since my mum was a girl, yet my grandmother still thought my fate should be the one she had wanted for her daughter. If I were married off, I would be respectable – and the family would also gain a few cows in the process.

I tried to make myself look as young as I could. As the months turned into years, I disguised my changing body as best I could. Thank goodness my sisters were too young for it to be an issue for them! In the village, I saw other girls who I knew were just 12 years old – yet they were married and pregnant. They didn't look happy about it either. I worked out for myself that starting your periods and becoming a woman was no cause for celebration. It made you a target.

In the rural, closeted lakeside community, there were no soldiers out to attack us. Instead, the threats were personal and faced by every young girl.

'Please let Mum come back soon,' I'd add to my secret night-time prayers. 'I'm not safe here.'

3

BANANAS ARE MY BUSINESS!

By working all the hours God sends, Mum finally got together enough money to be able to care for us once more. After about six months, we returned to our home in town. The political situation in Uganda had improved, although it was still volatile. What I cared most about was returning to school. I was so eager to learn! Mum was eager too – whenever my end of term reports came out, she'd cook a 'real' meal – one with meat or fish in it and tell me that, if my report was good, I'd be able to eat the food. Otherwise, only my sisters would! Of course, Mum couldn't actually read the reports I brought home, but she seemed to have a knack for working out if I wasn't saying out loud, verbatim, what the teachers had written down! I always got the special meal, though – I was an excellent student. I was particularly good at maths and athletics, where I excelled in the 100 metres.

The most challenging part of the school day for me was getting there. I'd walk the couple of miles barefoot and often cut my feet on broken debris. But that was nothing compared to the real danger – that I would be kidnapped on my way to school. The route from my home to school went past an army barracks, and soldiers would kidnap girls off the street. Some might be raped and abandoned. Others would be taken in to become a wife. This happened to several of my friends from school. These girls simply disappeared. And like those poor drowned pregnant women at Grandma's village, no one did anything about it. Families grieved for their loss. The authorities looked the other way. Each morning, we'd make sure we walked in groups. And we'd hold hands tightly so that the 'end girl' couldn't be picked off. It truly was that bad.

Always, I was scared. I walked fast. I kept my head down. This was what I had to do if I wanted to get educated.

Other families as poor as ours didn't send their children to school. You'd see them beg on the streets. I was able to attend school because of Mum's mission to improve our lives through education. At times, I was embarrassed to be the only girl in school with no shoes. 'Be strong,' I'd tell myself. 'Your teachers don't care how you dress – they care about what's in your brain.'

I'd give myself the same pep talk at lunchtime – my very worst time. When lessons broke up at midday, others in my class would eagerly open up their school bags to bring out their packed lunches.

Me? I'd open up my book.

I'd smell boiled eggs, fresh bread, spiced pastries – then I'd burrow my head back down into my book. My poor brave mother was making sacrifices so that I could attend school – she never bought herself clothes, and of course, she had no shoes either. It wasn't her fault that she couldn't provide any lunch. Heartbreakingly, I'd been sent into school without breakfast – and with the knowledge that my next (and only!) meal would be cheap starch at teatime. I was excited to learn, but being so hungry made it a struggle to find the energy to get through the day.

'You can share my eggs if you like,' one of the girls would sometimes say to me kindly. But I was way too embarrassed to take her up on her kind offer.

'Oh no, I'm not hungry today,' I'd lie, pushing her kindness away. 'I decided I'd spend the time reading, not eating.'

Mum had drummed into us not to accept things from others – no way were we to beg, like street children. So I felt I couldn't accept food from others, and my poverty became a barrier to friendships too.

And then, quite suddenly, my schooling stopped. I had passed P7, the final stage at primary school, and I had won a scholarship to a prestigious secondary school. I was so proud of myself!

'We don't have the money to buy the uniform or the books you'll need,' said Mum. 'I'm sorry Alice, you can't go. In fact, you may as well stop school right away.'

For Mum, because I could read and write (and much more than road signs!), I had achieved her target for me. It wasn't ideal, but she had done her best.

Besides, she now had four other children to focus on to: Phebby, her final daughter, and my brother Nicholas

Nicholas was given the second name Emanuel, which means 'God is now with us'. The thinking was that, because at last there is a boy in the family, God was finally with us.

I was devastated about having to stop school, but I was determined not to give up. Mum had shown me the importance of working hard, so I devised a plan. What if I could earn enough money to send myself to school? It was a crazy dream – I had no skills, and I was only 11 years old! Undaunted, I asked Mum to give me a very small amount of money so that I could buy mini bananas from the market and then sell them at a profit to individuals.

I'd seen other (older!) boys and girls do this and set off early for the market. What I hadn't factored in was just how cruel the marketplace is for a young, vulnerable child. I bought my bananas in bulk easily enough – but selling them, rather than having them stolen from me, was a daily battle.

I thought about how hungry I had been at school - and it occurred to me that other children would come out of their classes hungry too. Perhaps they would want my bananas? They certainly did – they swamped me and stole all my fruit. So I made a loss.

Other days were less bleak. I made enough money to buy a basket that – like my grandmother – I carried on my head. This worked better – but still, I was plagued by thieves. It was easy for adults who were taller than me to lean over and steal my bananas literally from over my head.

'Mum,' I said one evening, 'what can I do? This isn't working?'

Mum's ethos in life was that if Plan A doesn't work, you move on to Plan B. She remembered a group of missionary families that she'd known from her days working at the hospital. These families lived across town from us and worked for the Central African Tearfund. 'Why not try door-to-door sales?' she suggested.

I was nervous when I knocked on my first door. Would these people be suspicious of such a young girl? Would they think I was out to steal from rather than sell to them?

When Gill opened her door, her toddler hid behind her skirt. The family had recently arrived in Uganda, and I don't think her daughter had seen any local children before.

'Yes, I'll buy some bananas,' said Gill. 'But you look so tired and thirsty – why not come in for a cup of tea too.'

A cup of tea! No one had offered such kindness to me before. I could not believe it. She also gave me more money than I had asked for.

'Why not ask what else she might need,' said Mum when I excitedly told her about it later.

Soon, I was bringing pineapples, melons, grapes and eggs too. And not just to Gill. 'My friend lives across the way,' Gill had told me on my second or third visit. 'I'm sure she'd welcome a reliable weekly delivery.'

I had customers! I was making, not losing, money.

Gill's family were so lovely. I'd come in and play with her children each week too. Then I started to show them how African families would bake bread using the stovetop, not the oven.

One day, Gill sat me down. 'Tell me, Alice, you are so very young. Why aren't you in school?'

I spilled out my story of how I'd gained the top scholarship to secondary school, yet we had no money, so I couldn't go. I also told her about what had happened to my uncle and how my brave mother kept going today with her five children to support.

'Oh, Alice,' she said through tears. 'Life shouldn't be like this.'

A few weeks later came the news that was to change my life.

I'd accompanied the family on a trip to view a home they were moving to some miles away. They'd wanted someone who spoke the local language to come in case they encountered any difficulties. Gill and her family were sitting on a sofa, holding hands, when I came into their front room. Gill did the talking: 'Alice, we have decided that you must go back to school and that we will pay your school fees.'

I could not believe what I had heard! I was so shocked I cannot to this day remember if I said 'thank you'. Truly, I hope that I did – because their kindness meant that a world beyond poverty would open up for me.

Mum had always been adamant that we weren't to accept hand-outs from others - not even food from other children at school, for example. But she was thrilled when I told her about this act of extreme kindness shown to me. They were good Christian people and what they were giving me didn't feel like charity, because they were offering an opportunity, not goods. This was no hand-out. I still had to go on and do the hard work and do well at school.

At Bishop Kivengere Girls' school, in Kigezi, Kable, I worked so very hard that, by the second year, I was awarded a full-fees scholarship. The school was run by missionaries and was so far from my home that I had to board. Within the school compound, we were safe from whatever dangers were out on the streets. As a boarder, I also had the personal benefit that full meals were included. With one less mouth to feed at home, Mum saved up to buy me shoes. My first pair, which Mum bought me when I was 13, was simple lace-up pumps. Now, I could run and walk even faster and cram even more into my busy days! Gill continued to cover essential school extras until, at age 18, I left following my A levels. Next up – college!

A girl like me was going to have a full college education. Incredible! I enrolled in a business studies course at what is now the Makerere University Business School in Kampala. My joy was immense!

4

NINE YEARS OF ABUSE

Just like my mother before me, by the time I was 19, I was caught up with the wrong man. I had swallowed the dream that a handsome man who appears charming must be a nice guy. He was a medical doctor (just like my father!), and our partnership had been arranged by his parents, who paid cows to my mother (who kept them in readiness to give to the family of Nicholas's future wife). I had been at college and had been recommended to his family as a good, capable young woman through another family that knew our family. This was how things worked then! Whilst she was very proud that I - a girl - was in college - mum (back then!) didn't think about my having a career. I did - but ~ my plans were derailed by the excitement of the idea of meeting a man and having my own home. Nathan and I didn't formally marry, so he was a partner, not a husband, but even so, I went into this believing that I had found my forever person with whom I would start a family and live happily.

I could not have been more wrong.

I don't know how I didn't fall pregnant, but I did not.

When babies don't arrive, Ugandan culture always blames the

woman. When, after a year or so, I was still not pregnant, this man took it out on me and channelled his anger into controlling every aspect of my life. From not letting me see friends and family to insisting that I must stay home – all the better to cook and clean – I cowered to his demands because I was frightened of him. Then, when he took a new job and moved us to another town, my sense of isolation increased.

After around four years, I did become pregnant, but very sadly miscarried at 12 weeks. It was such a taboo in 1990s Uganda not to produce a healthy, living baby, that his family shunned me – at the very time when I needed reassurance and comfort. I was too far from home now for my own mother to provide love and care, and whilst I could, of course, have written letters to her, she still wouldn't have been able to read them. At this time, I didn't think of leaving. I assumed that I was stuck. Like so many women before me, my life had become derailed. This sorry and sad reality was it.

Then, after a further two years, this brutal man laid it on the line. 'If you can't provide a child, I will seek another woman who can.' Still vulnerable and heartbroken over the miscarried baby, I sought refuge in work. I got a job in finance with BAT (British American Tobacco). During office hours, at least, I could see and chat with other people. One evening, I returned home to find that our home had been cleared out. Even the bed had been removed.

After nine years with me, he had gone to live with a woman who 'could give him children' and taken everything out of our flat. And he had left without saying a word. At work, somehow, everyone knew what had happened. I kept my head down through the humiliation – and turned to my bible.

The Lord is my shepherd; I shall not be in want. He restores my soul.

Psalm 23 fell open by accident and seemed to say it all.

It gave me the strength to keep on.

I believe the Lord also led me towards a friend, Stella. She'd been studying in the UK and was back in Uganda briefly. 'Why not come with me when I go back?' she said. 'Doesn't have to be a big deal. You could spend six months; further your studies a bit; see how it feels . . .'

Thinking it over, I talked through the idea with other friends. Incredibly, yet again, I was poleaxed by the generosity of others. A couple I knew from a university chapel agreed to long-term loan me the money for the flight to the UK.

It was only 3 p.m. when the plane touched down at Heathrow. Curiously, it was already growing dark. As I stepped onto the airport tarmac, a cold wind blew across my ankles.

What was I doing more than 6,000 miles from home? Suddenly, six months seemed like a very long time.

5

LOVING LONDON, LOVING LIFE

First impressions are not everything. After that cold, grey start, I loved London! The full colours of Piccadilly Circus and Leicester Square exploded into my orbit as I became a vibrant, relaxed young woman about town. By day, I studied to become a certified accountant (ACCA) at London College. By night, I'd go clubbing with my new university friends. I took a room in a shared house, and, to pay for it all, I filled every spare hour with working. Factories. Fruit picking. Food packaging. 'What do you have that has the most hours, for the longest time?' I'd ask. I didn't want to waste a moment! I met a lovely man, too, but sadly, after a few months with me, he went back to his home in America.

Six months rolled on . . . at the last thing I wanted to do was return to Uganda I'd send messages home via a local post office, and my sisters would read them out to Mum. By this time, I had begun work. From accounting departments at Westminster City Council to the Ministry of Defence, I loved my new professional working life!

I found out, quite by chance, that I was known as 'the woman who is always smiling'. I was waiting by the lift at the same time as

Ms Makepeace, one of the senior bosses. When she'd asked me how I always managed to be so cheerful, I told her my truth. 'I think back to the last thing that I am happy about. There is always something, and bringing that to mind keeps a smile on my face,' I said, smiling, of course, as I spoke!

'Well, Alice, I'd have to go back a long way to get a good memory,' was her reply. And it left me reeling. That someone as successful as her, who'd come from an easy, comfortable family, would find it difficult to remember happy times! It didn't seem possible. Yet, with all her advantages, she'd clearly been admiring me!

I think my candour touched her that day, and she certainly touched me. I understood that I was as worthy as the next person. If I wanted to, I could work hard and be the 'next' big boss like Ms Makepeace. Only I would be one that always smiled.

I found a new Bible verse to guide me as well: Jeremiah 29:11. *For I know the plans I have for you; plans to prosper you and not to harm you, plans to give you hope and a future.*

As my 30s sailed on, I continued to be a very happy woman. I'd made the UK my permanent home now, and just one thing was lacking: motherhood. Romances came and went, and yet I did not fall pregnant. Back in Uganda, Anna, Ruth – even little Phebby – became mothers. I resigned myself to a life without children.

I set up the Good Shepherd Network charity so that I might help other children instead. I'd kept in touch with a missionary couple, Alan and Tricia Bapty my mother had known from her days at the leprosy hospital. When Alan later returned to work in Uganda as a doctor we had become as close as if we were a part of their family! Now, I reached out to their children, Diana and John Perryman, who lived in Manchester . Together, we founded Bapty School in Uganda for vulnerable and street children. It admitted boys and girls, of course – but it's the girls that I especially wanted to help. I believe with a passion that no girl should grow up believing that she is worth so little that she isn't even worth educating. What my mother instilled in her girls – and I am proud to report that my sisters are also educated, professional women – I sought to pass on to other children. Among my highlights is visiting the school each year.

There was sunshine, not grey skies, when my mother saw England for the first time in 2012. I bellowed out, 'Mama,' as soon as I saw her, just like people back home would project their voices across the distance. For her part, Mum could not believe how I lived. It was the little things. She opened my wardrobe – clothes and shoes in multiple colours. She nosed into the fridge – food that would have fed us for weeks in Uganda sat carelessly on shelves, ready for me to choose which dinner I fancied.

I'd organised a mobile phone for Mum by this point, of course. She was at home in June 2014 when I told her that I now had a master's degree in finance from Leicester University – and how I'd just spent a day in the presence of royalty! By now, I'd got a senior job with the Red Cross finance team, and through that, I'd been invited to the Queen's garden party. It felt like a highlight of my life to be there. I keep the invitation to this day: a physical reminder of how a girl from the poorest background imaginable went on to be accepted into the very highest of UK society.

6

DOUBLE JOY, SINGULAR HEARTBREAK

'Make that a double burger, please – today I am celebrating!' I was sitting outside at a favourite restaurant in Little Venice, London, and the happy chatter of people enjoying a leisurely lunch blended with the distant chug of boats along the canal. I'd done a pregnancy test a few days earlier – and now the news I'd been waiting for all my life was beginning to sink in. I was 43, and I was pregnant! I took the first bite of my food and savoured my surroundings. I looked around and saw other families – mums pushed prams, kids on bikes whizzed along the towpath. No one here appeared frightened or sad as I had been through my impoverished childhood in a dangerous, war-torn country. As I enjoyed my lunch, I watched boys *and* girls laughing in equal measure. I thought wow, how wonderful it would be to raise my child here!

It was a few months on when the full irony of my menu choice that day hit me. A double burger. Absolutely the right option for a woman expecting two babies!!

My twin pregnancy progressed without drama, and I arranged with Mum that she would fly over a few days before my due date. I was single by this time, but that was OK. I held a secure job and would easily be able to support my new family. I gathered all the equipment that two new babies might want and waited for Mum to arrive.

A friend came to my door with the news at around 7 a.m.

'You need to let me come in, and we must both sit down,' she said. The previous day, my incredible, beloved mother had been bustling about getting ready for her trip when she'd had a fall. At the hospital, her body went into shock – and they'd been unable to save her. She had died the same day.

It is impossible to put into words the depth and breadth of my grief. I would never see Mum again. I had kept back from her the amazing news that I was carrying a boy and a girl – the ultimate dream. I had wanted her to see their beautiful tiny faces and see that news first-hand for herself. And now she had died not knowing.

The next week was a blur. As an older mum with twins, I had an elective caesarean booked. But I could scarcely think about that. I sobbed on the phone with my sisters. Mum's funeral took place without me. It was the most wretched of days.

In the operating theatre, everyone knew about Mum. 'You are being really brave,' I was told. Abigail Florence arrived first (weighing 2.2 kilos) and named after my mother Florence; a minute later, and at 2.5 kilos, Joshua Samuel entered the world. Bringing my babies home a few days later was heaven. After waiting so long, how could I not be a natural mum?! I cocooned in with my newborns– feeding, sleeping, bathing and cuddling up close. I was living the dream!

After their three-month immunisations, I decided it was safe to take them to Uganda. Two infants, one mum and two connecting flights don't make for the easiest journey, but I had to see Mum's grave. I couldn't get a direct connection, so I spent 12 hours in the air and had to endure a stop-over change ... with my double buggy and tiny babies to steer through the concourse and through security. It was not pleasant I stayed with my sisters in Kabale, and part of me didn't want to leave – then, as now, it is Uganda that I call home. Despite all the hard times I experienced as a child, there is a sense of place that never leaves you. And, of course, I have always missed my sisters and brother. But now, I had two little people whose future rested on my decisions. I had to be practical: their very best future lay in London.

'We'll visit soon,' I told Phebby as she took me to the airport. She drove us, of course – in 2020s Uganda, educated, professional people like my sisters have cars and live in comfortable homes that they share with husbands that they have chosen on their own terms. Phebby has four children and is training to be a doctor. That I was the forerunner for my youngest sister to achieve so much brings true joy.

7

THE POWER OF POSITIVITY!

The first six years of my twins' lives have whizzed past in a blur of happy milestones. They are clever, kind children who engage fully at school and also soak up the extra-curricular challenges of swimming and music lessons that I line up for them. Six months ago, I achieved another milestone: I bought my first property – a flat in fashionable St John's Wood, London. Now my little family feels anchored and secure! I love that Abigail plays football (in Uganda, it is *still* just for boys!) and that Joshua can home-bake and be cuddly and snuggly just like his sis! This summer, I plan to take them to Uganda. It's important to me that they know their heritage. Besides, they have 19 cousins to meet.

At work, I am in the final stages of a master's degree in humanitarian shelter coordination with Oxford Brookes University. I am excited about a field trip to Geneva as part of this. In time, I would like to move into more humanitarian work. NATO? Who knows! I have discovered that anything is possible where there is self-belief underpinned by hard work.

It was a contact I made through a mum at the school gates who urged me to write this book. 'Your story is extraordinary; you have to share it,' Cindy Law told me. We'd met at a marketing show organised by her daughter-in-law, who has twins the same age as mine. Cindy, who is American, runs a charity herself and is an inspiring woman.

Later that evening, when Joshua and Abigail were scrolling on their iPads, and I was loading their lunchboxes into the dishwasher, I thought back on her words. I thought back on my childhood when I walked barefoot to school across several miles of rough ground – how I risked being kidnapped by groups of marauding soldiers in order to reach the school building – and how I'd sit hungry through the day, with just my determination to learn to sustain me.

Yes, I thought – my journey from there to my life today. I do have a story worth sharing.

I am sure it is because of what has happened to me that I believe that even if you have the odds stacked against you – with positivity and by staying focussed, you *can* pursue whatever it is that you most want in life. Once I was educated, I knew it was no longer true that I would 'amount to nothing'.

If you are facing hard times right now, I would say to you that there is no tunnel that doesn't eventually end in light. There may be rejections and scenarios that don't work out; failing to become pregnant was the biggest one for me. Yet, if you keep on trying, things *can* change.

I am 50 now, and to that core positivity, I would add, 'you are never too old!' I was a late mum. My sister Phebby is nearly 40, and, as I said earlier, it is only now that she is beginning her study to be a doctor.

My incredible, amazing mother had a zeal to get her girls an education. When Plan A didn't work, she moved on to Plan B, then Plan C. I can recommend no better approach. Wherever you are on your personal journey through life – I wish you success.

ABOUT THE AUTHOR

Alice Kyarimpa was born and raised in the South-Western Region of Uganda, known as the pearl of Africa due to the beauty of natural wonders . She grew up in a small town called Kabale near Bwindi impenetrable Forest a home of some of the last mountain gorillas on earth. Alice moved to London for greener pastures to complete her studies in Accounting and Finance.

Alice became a mother of twins in her late 40's. Something that she has come to know and love is that your future is determined by how you act in the present moment. Your past does not have to define you or your future.

In her free time Gorilla trekking is her hobby as their home is her backyard and she loves traveling and discovering new places.

Printed in Poland
by Amazon Fulfillment
Poland Sp. z o.o., Wrocław